each breath
a smile

Plum Blossom Books
P.O. Box 7355
Berkeley, CA 94707
www.parallax.org

Plum Blossom Books, the children's imprint of Parallax Press, publishes books on mindfulness for young people, parents, and educators.

Based on the teachings of Thich Nhat Hanh, this book was written by Sister Susan and illustrated by Nguyen Thi Hop and Nguyen Dong.

Summary: Children learn how to connect with their breathing to help them experience calmness and enjoy a deeper relationship with their friends and family and the world around them.

13 / 17

each breath a smile

Based on teachings by
Thich Nhat Hanh

Story by Sister Susan

Illustrated by Nguyen Thi Hop & Nguyen Dong

Dear little ones,
let us sit very quietly.

Listen...

Listen to the wind.

Listen to the birds.

Listen to the crickets and the frogs.

Listen very quietly
to your breathing.

Let us put our hand on our tummy
and feel our breathing.

Our tummy goes out
and then it goes in.

Breathing in
and
breathing out.

Our tummy goes out
and then it goes in.

Breathing in
and
breathing out.

I close my eyes and stay with my breathing in.
I close my eyes and stay with my breathing out.

It is so wonderful to feel my breath coming in.
It is so wonderful to feel my breath going out.

Breathing in, I calm my whole body.
Breathing out, my whole body is calm.
Body, calm.

Breathing in, I am blooming like a flower.
Breathing out, I feel fresh.
Flower, fresh.

Breathing in, I see myself as a mountain.
Breathing out, I feel solid.
Mountain, solid.

Breathing in, I see myself as space.
Breathing out, I feel free.
Space, free.

Breathing in, I come back to myself.
Breathing out, I smile.

Breathing in, the world is so beautiful.
Breathing out, I smile.

The blade of grass is so green.

The sky is so blue.

I see that
Mommy is lovely.

I see that
Daddy is wonderful.

I see that my sister is so kind.

I see that my brother
is so playful.

I see that my grandma and my grandpa are so sweet and gentle.

I see that my classmates
and my teacher
make me
so happy.

We listen

and we see

that all life
is breathing
with us.

PLUM BLOSSOM
BOOKS

Plum Blossom Books, the children's imprint of Parallax Press, publishes books on mindfulness for young people, parents, and educators. For a free copy of our catalog, please write us or visit our website:

Plum Blossom Books
P.O. Box 7355
Berkeley, CA 94707
www.parallax.org
Tel: (800) 863-5290

A Note to Parents and Teachers

Mindfulness is being present each moment of the day, being aware of what is happening here and now. A good way to practice mindfulness is through conscious breathing. It can enrich the interaction between adults and young children, encourage deep listening, and help reconnect to the wonders of life.

About the Authors

Thich Nhat Hanh is a Vietnamese Zen master who lives in exile in Plum Village, France. Nominated for the Nobel Peace Prize by Dr. Martin Luther King, Jr., he is one of the most beloved spiritual teachers of our times. Since 1983, he has lectured and led many retreats in North America and around the world on the practice of mindful living. He is the author of over fifty-five books in English, including *Living Buddha, Living Christ*; *Peace Is Every Step; Being Peace*; *Teachings on Love*; *Anger*; and three other books for children.

Sister Susan, ordained in the tradition of Thich Nhat Hanh, lives and works at Green Mountain Dharma Center in Vermont. She is very grateful for the practice and joy of mindful breathing and has a wholehearted wish that it will benefit children as well.

About the Illustrators

Nguyen Thi Hop and **Nguyen Dong** were both born in Vietnam. Since their marriage in 1968, they have collaborated on illustrations for thirty titles published in Vietnam, Japan, Germany, France, and the United States. Their illustrations also appear in another children's book by Thich Nhat Hanh, *A Pebble for Your Pocket*.

About Practice Opportunities

Families and children are especially welcome at the Plum Village Summer Opening, where monastics and lay people practice the art of mindful living. For more information, please visit www.plumvillage.org or contact:

Plum Village
13 Martineau
33580 Dieulivol, France
info@plumvillage.org

Blue Cliff Monastery
3 Mindfulness Road
Pine Bush, NY 12566
www.bluecliffmonastery.org

Deer Park Monastery
2499 Melru Lane
Escondido, CA 92026
Deerpark@plumvillage.org